MW00770791

The team at Life Suc̶ want to learn your dr̶e̶a̶m̶.̶.̶.̶ ̶.̶.̶.̶,̶ ̶, because once they help you document your dream and help you get started with your family banking process, then they'll be working to help make your dream a reality . . . and you might end up like I did with horses, a barn, and a pasture . . . one of our family dreams realized. Thanks to the help of Life Success & Legacy.

—David Shirkey
Director of Strategy at Orbitform

This is a story of financial hope and inspiration. This story combats the "Decision Fatigue" from all the financial noise that is out there. "Family Banking with Purpose" is a great place to RENEW or BEGIN receiving a different PERSPECTIVE of where you are now and instigate your IMAGINATION of what will become of your Story with money for you and your family.

Start waving HELLO to a reality of greeting your hopes and dreams in celebration.

—Winnie Lau (Canada) -
Authorized IBC Practitioner since 2010
Author of Cash Smart for Life
CEO of Empowered Life Financial Inc.

Get this book, read it, and implement it so you can achieve financial prosperity! The simple life lessons taught in this book can bring financial peace and harmony to any family. Finally, a story that shows the importance and value of real conversations about money in the family that can help more than one generation be successful. This is how you make your family just like the Rockefellers.

—Richard Canfield,
CEO of Ascendant Financial

One of the powerful pieces in our financial journey has been the teaching and coaching we've had from Chris and the Life Success & Legacy Team. It is no exaggeration that their training has changed our lives for the better.

— Ron Swall

We have had the deeply impactful blessing of being mentored directly by Mike, Chris, and the LSL team. Their genuine nature in teaching this message is something we will forever be grateful for. We are utilizing this book for our clients and our own investment journeys.

—Brandon Goswick,
CFO Unlimited Life Concepts
Nate Dean, CEO Unlimited Life Concepts

The guidance and support that Chris, Mike, and the team provided empowered us to take charge of our financial future, "turning our wind currents," and even propelling us to early retirement with guaranteed passive income. What a tremendous difference it has made for us!

—Michael Kwong, J.D., MBA, M.Ed

A powerful and touching story that turns conventional financial wisdom on its head. It opens the reader's mind to a whole new way to think about financial freedom.

—Kathy Tagenel
Cofounder of The Go-Giver Community
President of Zoom Strategies, Inc.

FAMILY
BANKING WITH
PURPOSE

A Story about Financial Freedom
through Infinite Banking

CHRIS BAY

King Publishing

Family Banking with Purpose: A Story About Financial Freedom
Through Infinite Banking

Chris Bay

Published by King Publishing

Copyright © 2021 by Chris Bay

All rights reserved.

King Publishing

E-mail: FamilyBanking.KP@gmail.com

Limit of Liability/Disclaimer of Warranty:

Publishing and editorial team: Author Bridge Media,
www.AuthorBridgeMedia.com
Project Manager and Editorial Director: Helen Chang
Publishing Manager: Laurie Aranda
Cover design: Tamian Wood

Library of Congress Control Number: 2021906475
ISBN: 978-1-7369611-9-3 -- Paperback
978-1-7369611-8-6 -- Hardback
978-1-7369611-7-9 -- ebook
978-1-7369611-6-2 -- audiobook

Ordering Information:

Quantity sales. Special discounts are available on quantity purchases by
corporations, associations, and others. For details, contact the publisher at
the address above.

Printed in the United States of America

DEDICATION

I dedicate this book to you, the reader.

May this story and the principles in these pages inspire you to dust off those old dreams for yourself, and encourage others toward their dreams as well.

CONTENTS

ACKNOWLEDGMENTS

This idea of writing a book has been peeking around the corners of my aspirations for many years. I would like to thank some special people who have played a role in encouraging this book to reality.

First and foremost, to my wife, Shawn (my pixie firecracker), who casually said to me late one night as I was reading about IBC, "I think you'd be good at teaching that." Your encouragement, support, and belief in me has provided validation, courage, and love as we have partnered in this journey hand in hand. Thank you.

To two amazing young women by whom I'm called various versions of "Dad," which I infinitely treasure, thank you. Lily, who is the true writer in the family, provided me frequent "You're doing great, Dad" encouragements throughout the process. Addie, who is an endless source of parodies of me teaching IBC, made me laugh until my sides hurt. To both of you, our Family Bank is for your present pursuits and future dreams.

My parents, who modeled vision, planning, and discipline and pursued their dreams even though they had little to no head start . . . which they provided me: thank you. I am ever aware of and forever grateful for the choices and sacrifices you have made for my family and me.

This book would never have been possible without the mentorship, friendship, and encouragement of my business partner, Mike Everett. Our diametrically opposed personalities could never work together if it were not for our mutual respect and love for one another. Thank you for allowing me to be me as we serve others together.

Thank you to friends and teammates Michael Crawford and Shelley Forbis. Your commitment to our purpose and representation of Life Success & Legacy is exceptional. To an even greater extent, I value your friendship and the manner in which you serve others.

The legacy Nelson Nash has provided us has the opportunity to ripple across the generations. His book *Becoming Your Own Banker* was the inspiration for this book. I will forever remember one of his visits to Lawrence, Kansas, and how during a private dinner with our team and family members he took a special interest in and engaged my young daughters, learning about their interests. I wish you all could have known Nelson—a kind and learned sage whose life is an example to me and so many others. Thank you, Nelson.

Finally, I express great gratitude to Helen Chang, Laurie Aranda, Iris Sasing, and the Author Bridge Media team for your creative guidance, editorial expertise, and publishing services. I grew to anticipate and appreciate how you would take my preconceived idea of the story and gently turn it on its ear, essentially "moving my cheese" and throwing my linear and sequential mind a curveball. That was fun! Your experience and proven process added context, depth, and so much more to the story I was hoping to tell.

INTRODUCTION

How do you save for retirement when half your income is going to taxes and debt repayment? You dream of leaving a financial legacy for your kids, but you have no idea how to do it. You're fighting against the headwind of a financial system that's not designed to help you be successful.

Market crashes can wipe out 401(k)s. Interest rates are at an all-time low, and college tuition is at an all-time high. For you, saving more means giving up more. Where do you go to learn better financial literacy? You're hopeless, frustrated, angry. You fear that you'll outlive your money.

You need a way out. You need an Infinite Banking Concept system.

In this parable, Rick and his wife are frugal with their money, but they're struggling to save for the future. When Rick's father passes away and his mother is left struggling, it seems like things will turn out even worse—until Rick's estranged grandfather introduces Rick to a new way for his family to eliminate their debt, create cash flow, and earn financial freedom.

Everything you need to create the life you want is available to you. You just need the tools.

Chapter 1

A FAMILY MATTER

Lesson 1: You are not alone.

Rick's tie felt too tight, but he couldn't reach up to fix it. His left arm was around his mother. On his right side, his wife, Meg, held his elbow. He stretched, flexing his neck instead of pulling on the tie, resisting the urge to look to his right. The casket felt like a magnet, trying to steal his attention.

He was here to bury his father.

At fourteen and twelve, respectively, his son, Cooper, and daughter, Julie, were old enough to understand death but young enough that the long funeral procession was overwhelming. Meg had sent them to sit in the pews while Rick and his mother shook hands with people and thanked them for coming. Rick's father, Kevin, was only sixty-two when he passed away from diabetes, and there had been a steady stream of well-wishers. The crowd included his old coworkers, his friends from the adult kickball league (Rick couldn't believe how popular it had become), and, of course, family.

A tall shape lumbered up from the line, and Rick stiffened. The old man in front of him looked a lot like Rick's dad but might as well have been a stranger. The man, who wore an old, worn-out suit and mismatched tie, twisted a cap awkwardly between his hands. "Hi, Rick," he said.

"Grandpa Bruce," Rick paused. He could feel the tension radiating off the women on either side of him. "This is my wife, Meg."

His wife, normally so socially adept, was too stunned to say anything.

"You can call me Bruce. Nice to meet you," Bruce said. His huge hand dwarfed Meg's as they shook.

"You too," she said. "Thanks for coming." As Bruce moved off into the crowd, Meg leaned in toward Rick. "How is it that you've never mentioned your grandfather? I thought he was dead."

Rick didn't answer. He didn't really know why his grandfather had never been a part of his life. All he knew was that his dad and Bruce had had a falling-out long before Rick was born. He wasn't surprised that the man had come to the funeral, but it felt strange to have him here. Kevin, twenty-four years younger than his father, was in the ground, but Bruce seemed to still be going strong.

Lawrence was a small city in Kansas, the kind of place where people still said hello on the streets. Rick lived in a subdivision near the university, and he had offered to host the reception so his mother wouldn't have to worry about cleaning up afterward, and so she could leave early if she wanted to. The four-bedroom house had a large open-concept living/dining room, so there was plenty of room for all of the people who followed them back after the funeral was over.

Almost everyone had brought food. Meg, her blue eyes sparkling, her short blonde hair messy and natural, took over with her usual warm humor and ran around keeping everyone organized. Every once in a while, her Chuck Taylor shoes would poke out from under her long black funeral dress. Rick moved from group to group, hearing stories about his dad, sharing some of his own. He had done his crying privately, days ago, but more than a few people shed tears on his shoulder.

"Hey, Uncle Buddy," Rick said, stopping beside a fit and lean older man. Uncle Buddy had a shark's smile and a wicked sense of humor. Rick and Buddy had never been close, but he was more a part of the family than Rick's grandfather.

"Buddy, please," his uncle reminded him.

Rick laughed. "You sound like Bruce," he said.

"Did you see he came?" With his chin, Buddy gestured toward the dining room, where Bruce chatted with someone Rick recognized as a childhood friend of his dad's. A few other people were with them, plates of finger food and glasses of wine in front of them.

Rick nodded. "Yeah, Meg nearly lost her mind. Had no idea he lived in town." He didn't add that his wife had no idea the man was even alive.

"How's your mom?" Buddy asked.

Rick sighed. "Worried. Dad didn't leave a lot. He was planning on working another seven years at least, paying off some debt. Now she's got the funeral, the medical bills . . ."

Buddy nodded. "That's hard."

"We'll do what we can, but—two kids, a mortgage. We're not much help." Rick shrugged. From across the room, he heard the sound of Meg's telltale laugh, the one he called "the cackle." It couldn't quite make him smile the way it usually did.

"You should talk to Bruce about that," Buddy said.

Rick snorted. "Bruce? Why? He's barely been in

our lives. He's not going to give his daughter-in-law any money."

"No, no, I mean advice. You'd be shocked at what he knows about money. It's made a huge difference for me—my family, my business, leaving something for my grandkids."

"Who would have thought!" Rick said, but he had no interest in talking to his estranged grandfather about money troubles. "Well, anyway, I should go check on Mom."

"Just come over and say hi," Buddy suggested, and without waiting for an answer, he made a beeline for the table. Reluctantly, Rick followed.

Buddy introduced Rick to the other three people at the table. Susan and Mike were childhood friends of Kevin's, and Rick remembered them a little. Donald, their father, lived two farms down from Bruce and was a good friend of his.

"How was Fiji?" Buddy asked Mike as he sat down. Rick took a seat across from his grandfather, giving him a nod that Bruce returned.

"Great! I did a little business and wrote off half the trip. Paid for the entire thing with an IBC loan." He lifted his glass in a silent toast, and Buddy laughed and clinked Mike's glass with his own.

"I thought you were a teacher," Rick said to Mike.

"I was, but I quit. Always wanted to start my own business, and it's doing so well that I travel half the year now. Thanks to Bruce, I have cash-flow freedom." Mike smiled at Bruce, who brushed the compliment away with a sharp wave of his huge, wrinkled hand.

Though unsure of how Bruce could have made that happen, Rick smiled and nodded along.

"Thank God for IBC," Donald agreed. "What a weight off my shoulders!"

Everyone nodded. Rick hadn't heard the term before, but he smiled along with everyone else. Susan offered Rick a mini quiche, which he took gratefully. He had been too busy to eat.

"Have you been using new money or policy loans for your premium deposits?" Buddy asked Mike.

"Half-half," Mike said. "I'm still funneling money over from an old fund my dad had started."

Rick was surprised at the tone of the conversation. When his own friends talked about finances, it was all complaining. Mortgage rates, credit card bills, the cost of children. He didn't even know what IBC and premium deposits were. "What do you do?" he asked Susan.

She laughed. "Oh, not much these days. I worked

in medical services, but now, I guess . . . I'm sort of into banking."

"What about you?" Donald asked Rick.

"Oh, I'm an administrator at a university. Nothing exciting."

"What are your big dreams?" Susan asked.

Rick thought about how many of his dreams had died over the years. He thought about how reality had taken over, how the need to provide for his family had pushed so much of that to the background. He thought about debt and the sleepless nights that came with it. But all he said was, "I guess just pay off my mortgage and save for my kids' college tuition."

"You'll get there for sure! I eliminated my outside debt in about seven years," Mike said. "It doesn't have to take long. I have to thank Bruce for showing me how."

Rick's eyebrows shot up. He couldn't stop staring at his grandfather. Bruce saw him looking and snorted a laugh through his thick white mustache.

"I told you," Buddy said. "Bruce has helped a lot of people achieve financial freedom."

My grandfather? Rick thought. He was a farmer! Did he really help all these people? Could I ever have financial freedom for my family?

Bruce smiled, and Rick found himself smiling back.

Maybe Buddy was right. Maybe Rick had an opportunity to learn from Bruce. And maybe Rick could even find out what happened between his father and grandfather all those years ago.

Later, as Rick helped Meg put away some of the dishes that had piled up around the house, he told her about the conversation at the table. She'd never heard of IBC either.

"Maybe this is the excuse you need to get to know your grandfather better," she said. "I want Cooper and Julie to get to know him too. He's family."

Rick piled the last of the plates on the kitchen island. "The man doesn't even want to be called grandfather."

"Talk to him. Before he leaves." She pushed her husband gently toward the door.

"And say what?" Rick asked. His wife could sense he wanted this. He had always cared about family, even if his own relationship with his dad had never been good.

"You'll think of something," she said.

Reluctantly, he left the kitchen. The last of their guests were putting on coats and getting ready to go. Bruce and Buddy stood by the coatrack, getting their stuff together. Rick jogged over a little too quickly because once he got there, he wasn't sure what to say.

"Thanks," he said. "For coming."

Bruce nodded gruffly. "We had our differences," he said. "But he was my boy."

"I wish . . ." Rick trailed off, unsure of how to finish the thought. How could he make a connection with this man, this stranger who shared his blood?

"I could use some help mending a fence," Bruce announced suddenly like this was a perfectly normal request. He said it like Rick helped him out all the time. "How would you like to come out to the farm on Saturday?"

"Yes!" Rick blurted out. He laughed self-consciously at his own enthusiasm. What the hell did he know about fixing a fence? "I'll bring my hammer."

Bruce laughed. "You do that." He put on his old, battered hat and went outside. Buddy nodded goodbye and followed him.

Rick took a deep breath and closed the door behind them. No matter what else happened, he felt less alone than he had when he put his father in the ground this morning. His family was still here, and maybe it wasn't too late to get to know them.

Chapter 2

TRAPPED IN A HEADWIND

Lesson 2: Life becomes simpler
when you control the wind current.

That Saturday, Rick left early for the farm. The only hammer he owned was small, and he was embarrassed to bring it. So he popped into the hardware store and picked up something heftier. While there, he ducked into Dick's Sporting Goods—just to look around—and saw a beautiful fishing rod on a great sale. He and Meg had promised to stick to a tight budget to pay down their debt, but he couldn't stand the restrictions. It was just a fishing rod, right?

True, he had five other fishing rods in the garage, unopened, with labels and price tags still attached. But he pictured himself out on the water, brim pulled low over his eyes, maybe with Cooper or Julie beside him . . . Next weekend, for sure. Or the one after. He bought the fishing rod and hid it in the back of the car so Meg wouldn't see it.

The drive to the farm wasn't long, but he had never been to his grandfather's house. It was a beautiful homestead overlooking six hundred acres on the Kansas River. Buddy and Bruce waited on the large wraparound porch, drinking coffee from large mugs.

As Rick got out of the car, he heard a loud sound and looked up in alarm, but it was only a plane flying low overhead.

"Morning, Rick!" Bruce called out after the engine noise had subsided.

"This is quite the place!" Rick said as he walked up the steps. The bristly old man swelled with pride.

"Damn right. Built in 1920, and I've done all the repairs in the original style. They've filmed two movies here." Bruce drained his coffee and pushed himself to his feet, indicating with a wave that Rick should follow.

Buddy joined them beside an old pickup truck. They all slid onto the bench seat, Bruce chatting about the history of the house and the old senator who had built it. Rick tried to imagine his father growing up on this farm, riding in this very truck by his father's side.

"So, how's work?" Buddy asked.

"Oh, you know," Rick said. "It's fine. I lead the technology support team at the university," he explained to Bruce. "It's good work, but there's a ton of bureaucracy and red tape. Nothing like this." He waved at the wide green fields around them, the open blue sky. "I'd love to run my own business, to have the freedom to be my own boss. But." He shrugged.

"But?" Buddy pressed.

"I have a mortgage," Rick said. "The kids' upcoming college tuition. I'm already busy paying off debt. I can't take the risk. You know how it is."

"Headwind," Bruce said with a bit of disgust.

"What?" Rick asked.

"Have you noticed those planes flying overhead?"

"Sure?" Rick said as if it were a question.

"Planes fly in all kinds of environments. Sometimes there's a headwind; sometimes there's a tailwind. Sometimes you get no wind at all. How fast the plane gets to where it's going all depends on the winds." He drummed his fingers on the steering wheel and looked over at his grandson. "You used to run those long races in high school, didn't you?"

"I didn't know you knew that," Rick said in surprise.

He'd been a marathon runner for years until life had gotten too busy.

"When you ran, did it make a difference which direction the wind was blowing?"

"Well, sure. If the wind was blowing hard into my face, I felt about ten years older than I was. With the wind at my back, I felt like I could fly."

Bruce pulled the truck over beside a length of fence that had seen better days. "You've got yourself a headwind with your finances. You're trying to finance your life and your retirement at the same time, and all on a single income."

"There's nothing I can do about that, though," Rick said in surprise.

"You know, most Americans are financing their lives with bank loans, student loans, and credit cards?" Bruce grimaced. "They're spending about 35 percent of their after-tax dollars just on the interest from their debt!"

Rick snorted. "None of my interest rates are that high. In fact, I've never heard of *any* interest rates that are 35 percent."

"But it isn't about the interest rate," Buddy explained. "It's the *volume of interest* over the life of the loan. Think about your mortgage. Ever noticed how much of your payment goes to interest and how much goes to the principal?"

Rick frowned as he started to catch on to what they were saying. "Yeah, we refinanced when interest rates dropped, and most of our new payment was interest."

Uncle Buddy nodded. "That's how they get you. In the first five years of a mortgage, you're paying *85 percent of the payment* to interest!"

"I knew it was high, but that . . ." Rick whistled. He was brought sharply back to a memory of talking finances with his father. Rick's mom and dad had been experts at stretching a dollar. But talking with Bruce and Buddy felt different to him. It felt like they had information no one else had.

Bruce and Buddy hopped out of the truck, and the three men moved equipment from the back of the pickup over to the fence. Rick could see Bruce had been a strong man in his earlier years, but the years had taken their toll, and his hand shook as he handed over a large posthole digger. Rick moved quickly to take it.

"Rick, does that retirement plan at the university give you a decent return?" Bruce asked.

"Most years, it does pretty well. I think I'm getting around a 10 percent rate of return." Rick pulled the number out of the air. He had gotten so overwhelmed with the family finances that he had stopped paying attention to the minutiae years before. He was just hoping and praying that it would grow enough so he could retire someday.

Bruce pursed his lips. "Hmm. Is that an average rate of return or an annual rate of return? Is it before or after the management fees the company charges? Does that 10 percent take into consideration the taxes you'll have to pay when you start liquidating the money at retirement?"

Buddy laughed at Rick's expression and slapped him on the shoulder. "I think you've got some questions to ask on Monday morning," Buddy said. "For now, why don't we work on this fence and let some of this marinate?"

But Rick was keyed up and keyed in. There was so much to learn! "Hold up. I just want to know more about the taxes at retirement."

Bruce leaned onto the tailgate of the truck, settling in for a talk. "Let me ask you this. Do you think income taxes are going to go up or down in your future?"

Rick laughed. "Up, definitely."

"Okay then. Do you think the value of a dollar will go up or down?"

That was an easy one. "Down, for sure. I remember

being able to buy a bottle of coke for twenty-five cents when I was a kid."

Bruce rocked back on his heels. "Since we're at the farm, I'll ask a farming question. Would you rather pay taxes on the 'seed,' the little amount, or the 'harvest,' the big amount?"

"Well, the seed, of course!" Rick said.

Bruce grinned a shark smile. "With your retirement at the university, you'll pay taxes after you retire, on the harvest. But taxes will most likely increase, and the value of the dollar will decrease. So you'll be paying higher taxes on the harvest and gaining access to dollars that are worth less than they are today." He paused to let that sink in.

"Meanwhile, after you pay about 30 to 40 percent to income, property, and sales tax, you're losing an additional 35 percent of your dollars on the interest on your debt. That money's just gone to the loan sharks. So, last question. Would you rather have the 10 percent return on your retirement plan you have now, which grows slowly but takes some hits, or have the 35% percent you're sending out the door on your debt?"

Rick was hesitant to answer this time. "Is this a trick question? I mean . . . obviously, I'd rather have the 35 percent, right?"

His grandfather took pity on him. "You're not alone. Most people are fighting the headwind of interest on their debt. What they need is to control the environment and create a tailwind. They need to bank with a *purpose*." He leveraged himself up from the tailgate and stretched. "Okay, gentlemen, let's get started on the work at hand."

Soon all three men were digging and clearing scrub. Once they had settled into a rhythm and the work came more easily, Rick picked up the thread of the fallen conversation. "You said it's up to people to create a tailwind," he said. "But how does that happen?"

Though the question had been directed at Bruce, it was Buddy who answered. "You have access to an amount of money. A pool. The size of your pool depends on how much you deposit into it and the pool rules."

Bruce joined in. "Your retirement plan at the university is a pool, and you're funding it like you're supposed to. But the 'pool rules' aren't in your favor."

Rick was starting to regret his retirement plan. "So what are pools of money that other people access?"

Buddy glanced up, squinting against the bright sun. "Savings accounts, CDs, 401(k)s, life insurance. But they all have pool rules to keep in mind. Some allow loans, which will have an interest rate applied to the loan and will decrease the balance and, thus, the return on the money. Some will limit the number of loans you can take to one or two at a time. You would have to pay back the entire loan before being able to take another loan. In most cases, 'they' control the terms of the loan . . . the pool rules."

Rick's head was starting to spin. And why had Buddy mentioned life insurance? Rick had always heard that was the worst place to put your money. "Okay, I'm guessing the two of you have some experience with all of this. Could you skip to the answer? What pool is the best to create and control?"

Bruce chimed in with his characteristic smile. "We've still got an hour or two of work left. If we give you all the answers right off, how will we entertain ourselves?"

Rick chuckled. "Great. I'm glad I can distract you."

Pausing from his hammering, Bruce wiped his arm across his forehead and took a moment to catch his breath before he spoke. "Rick, this may go against everything you've ever learned about money. But if you're willing to engage in this learning, I can show you how to create a pool of money that you control. That pool will not only help you start to turn your wind current, but it'll create a system that will benefit Cooper and Julie, and even their kids."

Rick walked back to the truck and got a drink from his water bottle, mulling it over. "You know, I always talked with my dad about finances, and the things we talked about lined up with what the financial gurus said. And those things are so different from what I've heard from you and Buddy. But what I've been doing up to this point doesn't seem to be working. Money is one of the only things Meg and I fight about. So I guess I don't have anything to lose in learning a different way. Plus, Bruce, I've enjoyed getting to know you a little better. I thought . . . next time we get together, I could learn a little more about my dad, too, if you'd be okay with that."

Bruce smiled. He crinkled his nose and looked away, hiding his emotion. "You've got yourself a deal."

All three men went back to work. Soon the fence had been repaired, and they were congratulating each other and packing up, ready to go back to the farm for a good, hearty meal. As Rick handed over the last of the equipment that needed stowing, Bruce asked, "How's Shelley doing?"

Rick sighed. "Mom seems . . . hopeless, and I've never seen her like that before. Not even when Dad was diagnosed with diabetes. She's struggling with finances. Thinking about going back to teaching full time or maybe selling the house. I'm just not sure how she's going to make it work. And we're not much help. We already have no margin."

Bruce and Buddy both shook their heads in empathy. "If you're comfortable sharing, I would like to keep up with how Shelley's doing," Bruce said. "I've always been especially fond of her."

Rick nodded. "Of course, Bruce." The old man clapped him on the back and headed for the truck.

As Rick slid into the cab of the truck next to Bruce, his grandfather looked over at him fondly. "I've always had a knack for picking winners," he said. "I'm banking on you."

Chapter 3

THE COUNTY FAIR

Lesson 3: Get multiple uses of your dollar.

The Douglas County Fair was a good old-fashioned family experience. Baking competitions, food trucks, and rides for the kids took place right alongside animal shows, barrel races, and riding competitions. Rick and Meg had taken the kids to the fair when they were little, but it had been years since they had gone. It seemed like the perfect place to introduce them to their great-grandfather for the first time.

At age fourteen, Cooper was shy and spent most of the time staring at his phone, but Julie, twelve, had all kinds of questions for her family. She chatted Bruce's ear off about wanting to become a veterinarian and asked him all kinds of questions about the animals on his farm. He showed her and Cooper how to feed the goats with their hands flat so they wouldn't get nipped and dragged them all over to see the bucket calves and other animals on display.

The owners walked the animals into the competition ring, following the judges' instructions. Buddy, who had been judging a competition, came down to meet the rest of the family, and everyone hugged.

"I didn't know you were into all this," Meg said to Buddy.

"Oh, sure. I'm not a full-time farmer like Dad, but we did some 4-H when I was growing up. Dad used to make Kevin and me shovel the manure." He laughed.

"Buddy, come on the Octopus with me!" Julie gaped at the orange arms of the ride rising above them.

Buddy laughed. "No, no. I'm an old man, kid. Take your mom."

"Thanks for volunteering me," Meg joked. "Would you three go get us some food?"

"You got it." Rick kissed her lightly, and she took the kids over to the games area while Rick, Buddy, and Bruce wandered toward the food trucks. As they passed the carnival, Rick saw a familiar game: a child's swimming pool full of little yellow ducks. People were throwing rings into the pool, trying to get one over a duck's head. It reminded him of the conversation he had on the farm.

"If only making money from my pool was as easy as tossing a ring!" he joked, directing the men's attention to the pool.

"Those games are actually a lot like your retirement plan. The only person who really wins is the person who owns the pool," Buddy said with a laugh.

"True," Rick said.

"That's why, if you want financial freedom, it's so important to create your own environment," Bruce said.

"You mentioned that the other day. I'd love to hear more?" Rick phrased it as a question. They chose a food truck selling walking tacos and funnel cakes and got in the long line.

"Well, it's pretty simple," Bruce said. "If we borrow money, we have to pay interest for the use of that money. But what people don't think about is, if we pay cash for our purchases, like buying a car, that cash is out of our control. We've completely lost the compounding interest on that money. Right?"

"Right," Rick said.

"You know, some have called compound interest the eighth wonder of the world," Bruce said. "By creating our own pool of capital, we can pay cash for our purchases and still never interrupt the compounding interest."

They reached the front of the line, and Bruce took out his wallet. He pulled out a twenty and waved it. "Most of us are getting only one use out of our dollars. We have to make a decision. Do I spend this dollar to pay down debt, invest for the future, pay my insurance premium . . . or buy these donuts?" He handed over the bill and took his mini donuts and coffee. "Well, there's a way to get multiple uses with the same dollar."

"Seems like magic," Rick said. He purchased walking tacos for the family and two funnel cakes to share.

"Not magic. Just pool rules," Bruce said. "You can make the pool a bunch of ways, but the rules are what make it work—or not. A specially designed whole life insurance policy from a mutual company is the most efficient way to create a pool you can use for your banking needs. Now, I'm going to guess that you may have heard somewhere that whole life insurance is the worst place to put your money."

Rick laughed. "I did have that thought when Buddy mentioned it last time we talked."

"When you deposit capital into a whole life policy that's designed to emphasize the cash value, which is the equity, and de-emphasize the death benefit, you gain three uses of your dollars: death benefit, growth that's guaranteed by contract, and loans against your policy to finance anything you want." Bruce ticked them off on his fingers.

Buddy joined in the conversation, coffee and sausage biscuit in hand. "I use my loans against my policy for a bunch of things. Works similar to a home equity loan. I've used it for home improvement projects, taxes, even loans to my business."

"And unlike a home equity loan, Buddy has total control over how and when he makes payments on that loan against his policy," Bruce explained.

Slowly they wandered through the fairgrounds toward the lazy arc of the Ferris wheel.

Bruce kept talking, his normally animated gestures hampered by the food in his hands. "When you take a loan against the policy, the guaranteed growth isn't a loan *from* the policy; it's a loan *against* the policy. It uses the cash value as collateral. If there's an outstanding loan after you pass, it's subtracted from the death benefit before the tax-free check is written to the beneficiary."

"So if I had a million-dollar policy, and I borrowed $100,000 to pay for college for the kids, when I die, Meg would get $900,000 instead of a million," Rick said.

"You got it," Buddy said. "And because of how life insurance is structured, when you take a loan against your policy, the company doesn't care if, or when, you make payments on your policy loan. You have total control and flexibility."

Bruce added, "Plus, you're only charged interest annually when the loan is initiated, and each year after that based on the remaining balance of the loan. That's a huge difference compared to credit cards. Those charge compounding interest each month."

"Wow. And we can gain three uses, right?" Rick asked.

"Right. Here's an example where you can gain three uses of your dollar." Bruce stopped to consider what he wanted to say. His eyes lit up as he thought.

Rick couldn't help but smile too. Bruce reminded him so much of his father.

They continued walking. "Let's say I pay my property insurance and property taxes once a year because I get a discount for paying annually," Bruce said. "If I pay those bills from my savings, I gain only one use of those dollars. Now, let's say I have an Infinite Banking Concept policy. Instead of paying my taxes, I use that money to pay the premium on the IBC policy, which gives me life insurance coverage. Those dollars are now growing and compounding without being at risk in the stock market. Lastly, without impacting the growth of my policy, I take a loan against my policy to pay my property insurance and taxes. I'm gaining three uses of the same dollars by doing it this way."

"That's incredible! You could do that with anything! Christmas gifts, vacations, education funds . . . It's like a really amazing savings account!" Rick was so excited he almost dropped the bag with the funnel cakes and quickly caught it. "Our use of money today can give purpose for the future," he mused quietly, almost to himself.

"And when Julie and Cooper go to college, for most schools, you don't have to list life insurance as an asset if they're applying for financial aid," Buddy said. "When my kids were in college, we used the financial aid to pay for school and put all our savings for tuition and housing into our IBC policies, where it grew for four years. Then the kids graduated and had to start making payments on the student loan balance. We just took a loan against the policy and paid down the student loan."

Rick finished his walking taco and tossed the bag and fork in the trash. They had reached the ride area, and he saw his family up at the top of the Ferris wheel. He waved, feeling like he was up among the clouds with them. The future seemed full of hope.

Rick turned to Bruce. "Last time we talked, you

told me 'I have a gift for picking winners. I'm banking on you.' Did you ever say that to my dad?"

Bruce sighed. He crumpled up his empty bag of donuts, thoughtful. "Kid, there are a lot of things I regret not telling your dad. He deserved more from me, but by the time I had some sense knocked into my head, I think too much damage had been done. My relationship with your dad is my greatest sadness."

"I think he felt the same way," Rick said.

Bruce looked up at that and nodded. "I did do some things right."

"I'd like to hear about those," Rick said.

"Maybe we can talk about that next time we get together." Bruce cleared his throat. "You like tacos? I know a great place in North Lawrence for Taco Tuesdays."

Rick smiled. "It's a deal."

Julie came barreling off the Ferris wheel, her mom and brother just behind, chattering about how she was pretty sure she could see their house, but Cooper insisted that was impossible because of the angle of the Earth's curvature. Rick and Meg shared a smile over their heads. It was great to have the family all together.

"Who wants funnel cakes?" Rick asked, to a resounding cheer.

Chapter 4

TACO TUESDAY

Lesson 4: Send everything you can
to your banking system.

A week later, Rick met Bruce at La Tropicana. A small family-owned restaurant in North Lawrence; it had a view of the train tracks and a huge outdoor patio. The hostess led Rick through the restaurant, where he caught a glimpse of employees in the kitchen rolling tortillas and grilling them over a round, open stove. Out back, colorful umbrellas and gigantic sycamore trees shaded black wrought-iron patio chairs and tables. A short adobe wall with bright blue, orange, and yellow tiles surrounded the area. Mariachi music played from the sound system.

Bruce had claimed a table in the corner. He stood, and Rick shook his hand before taking a seat across from his grandfather. It was the first time they had been alone together, and Rick was more nervous than he expected. "This is a great place," he said.

"It's been around since the mid-1900s. The family salsa recipe is the best I've ever had. Passed down through the generations of the Del Campo family. They've created a real legacy."

Bruce took a sip of his Mexican beer as Rick picked up his menu. A loud, sharp train whistle pierced the air, and a train rattled past, making conversation impossible. When the noise had faded, Bruce said, "It's just what I wanted to do for our family."

Rick looked at his grandfather in surprise. "A legacy?"

Bruce nodded. "When your Dad was a teenager, I was struggling to keep the farm afloat. Interest rates were high, and crop prices were down. I needed all the help I could get. Your dad and uncle worked long hours." He paused, toying with his menu, opening it and closing it again. "Buddy didn't mind so much, but Kevin . . . He wanted to play baseball. There was a team in town, but I needed him on the farm. Plus, we didn't have enough to pay for the uniform." He took another long swig of his beer, and when he spoke again, his voice was firmer. "Plus, I may have blown my fuse too many times. All I could talk about with your dad, or anybody else, was farm work. It consumed me."

The waitress stopped by, and Bruce let the story linger as they both ordered heaping plates of tacos. When she was gone, Rick gave Bruce his full attention. "I knew you two had problems, but Dad never talked much about what they were."

"By the time the farm was stable, too much damage had been done," Bruce sighed. "It was too late to rebuild the connection with your dad. I know he was hurt, but he showed up as a pissed-off teenager, and that anger never seemed to burn away."

Rick laughed, remembering his own stories. "That's Dad, all right."

"You probably know that when your dad started his own family, he wouldn't accept any help from me or your grandmother—may she rest in peace. Even so, I did some things right."

Another train rattled past going the other direction on a separate rail, blurring out his next few words, so Bruce paused until the train had passed. "When your dad and uncle Buddy were first born, I bought life insurance policies on each of them. They weren't anything special, and I didn't really know what I was doing, other than a friend of mine told me to buy whole life.

I funded them with new money each year. Even though the policies were small at the time, I was amazed at how the policies grew to be sizeable as each boy became a man. I saw the financial freedom I was building for the next generation. So I decided to do the same thing whenever a grandchild was born."

"Grandchildren?" Rick asked.

Bruce gave a mysterious smile. "That's right. When I turned sixty-five, after your dad had been married a good while and you were in your early twenties, I learned how whole life policies could be used to create a banking system like we've been talking about. From that point on, I started creating a banking system that I knew would help the family for generations to come, well after I was gone. I guess that's why it's called the Infinite Banking Concept. With IBC, I knew I could help your dad and your family, even if our relationship never mended."

"I'm sorry that it didn't. That you never got the chance to have this conversation with him." A warm breeze traveled through the restaurant, and Rick tilted his face into it with a smile.

Bruce folded a taco carefully in half as if folding his own emotions down at the same time. "Well, at least I can do this much for him. Those policies were always intended for your dad and his family. Now that Kevin has passed, it's only right that those proceeds be passed along to your mom, to help her."

Rick stopped, a taco halfway to his mouth.

"There should be enough to pay off the remainder of your mom's debt and the mortgage too," Bruce said.

Rick's eyes felt as wide as the tortillas left on his plate. "Bruce, I—are you sure? That's incredibly generous. You have no idea what that means to my mom . . . and me. She won't believe this. It will give her . . . real financial freedom!"

"It's your dad's inheritance, after all. I sold off some of my land and used the proceeds to build a banking system that would benefit our family for generations." Bruce coughed into his napkin. The cough was long and deep, and Rick watched him in concern, but Bruce just put the napkin down and took a sip of his beer as if nothing had happened.

"How does that work?" Rick said.

"You mentioned that money is a point of friction between you and Meg. I've heard it's the number one problem couples have. That sure was the case between your grandmother and me when the farm was struggling and before she passed away. What would you say about money is the most challenging for you and Meg?"

Bruce reached for the salsa, spooning some onto his last taco.

"I think the main thing is that since we have a single income, we only have a certain amount of money to work with," Rick said. "Meg really wants to pay down our debt, and I can see why. She's always wanting to send extra payments beyond our minimum to our credit card debt. Or she wants to make an extra payment on our mortgage to pay down the principal. On the other hand, *I'm* thinking about my retirement. I'd like to contribute as much as I can to that instead, but the reality is I'm seeing it get further and further away. It's hard to know which one to prioritize." Rick finished his root beer, setting the glass down on the tabletop.

"Well, I can tell you that we've all been taught to pay extra on our debt payments, but if you send that extra dollar toward the debt, we're only gaining one use of that money, and it's gone, never to be seen again. If you send the minimum payment and put the remaining amount into the IBC system, you'll gain multiple uses of those extra dollars. Then, you can take a loan against the policy and 'chunk' down on the balance of the debt. So, Meg is right that you want to pay beyond the minimum payment. But if you run it through your IBC policy, take a loan against your policy to pay down on the balance of the debt, you gain those three uses for your dollar."

"I can't wait to tell her about this. That's true for our mortgage too, right?"

"It definitely is," Bruce said. "Most people have heard they should get a fifteen-year mortgage if they can afford the monthly payments, so they can pay the loan off early and save on interest. But a thirty-year mortgage has a lower monthly payment. So, the difference between the two can be sent to your banking system. You gain three uses of those extra dollars, and then chunk down on the mortgage. Most people using their own banking system can pay off a thirty-year mortgage in less than ten years, all without changing their cash flow."

"They're just changing where their cash is flowing," Rick said in amazement.

Bruce laughed. "I like that. That's a good way to, say, send other people as little of your money as possible, and send your banking system as much as possible."

The waitress had come, and Rick covered lunch for both of them. It was the least he could do after everything Bruce was teaching him.

"You said you might want to own a business someday, didn't you?" Bruce asked.

"I'd love to," Rick admitted. "But I've been worried about getting the capital and losing my pension."

"You should talk to your Uncle about how IBC can help your business. He uses it in a lot of creative ways. One way is for his income taxes. Instead of sending the IRS quarterly estimated taxes, he stores his tax dollars in his policy, uses that money to pay his policy premium deposit, then takes a loan against his policy to pay his taxes once a year. He pays a small penalty for not paying quarterly, but it's worth every penny."

"There's so much to learn," Rick said, signing the check and leaving a generous tip. "It's a little . . . overwhelming. I don't know where to start."

"Let me give you some simple principles that will help." Bruce held up three fingers and ticked each one down as he spoke. "First, think long term. This is about creating a system for future generations, not just for yourself. Second, capitalize your system. In other words, if you want a little out of your banking system, put a little in. If you want a lot out of the system, put a lot in. And finally, *never* steal from your system. Be an honest banker, and make regular payments to your IBC system, just like you would at the bank."

Rick nodded. "Okay. I get it. Think long term, capitalize the system, and be honest." He took a breath that felt deeper than any breath he had taken in years. Finally, a road forward. He stood, and Bruce did the same.

"You already have a place to start, Rick. I took out a policy for you when you were just a baby. You may not remember, but I took out policies for Cooper and Julie too."

Rick vaguely remembered. "That's right. I remember having to sign some papers for you to start policies on the kids. At the time, I thought it was super weird, given that you weren't really in our lives."

Rick was stunned as it all came together for him. "I had no idea what all you were doing behind the scenes. Thank you." He hugged his grandfather. The old man returned the hug reluctantly and pushed Rick away with a gruff shake of his shoulder.

"Okay, okay. Come on," Bruce said with a devilish smile.

As the two men walked out of the restaurant, a lively woman thanked them for coming in a tone that showed she knew Bruce well.

"Adrienne, this is my grandson, Rick," Bruce said. It was the first time Rick had heard him say those words.

"Nice to meet you," Rick said, shaking her hand.

"I've heard so much about you from your

grandfather." Adrienne's deep booming voice was twice as big as her tiny frame. "It's so nice to finally meet you! I hope you come back with your family too. I'd love to meet Bruce's great-grandchildren."

Rick promised to do just that, and the two men headed outside.

"Like the La Tropicana family, we have a lot to pass down in this family," Bruce said.

Rick patted Bruce on the back. "More than I ever imagined."

"Wait till you see what my friend Jorge has done for his family," Bruce said with his wide toothy grin. "You'll really be inspired then!"

Chapter 5

A LESSON FROM JORGE

Lesson 5: Create a Family Bank
to recycle money.

The barn was large and white, with a long gravel driveway leading up to it. Everything—from the sweeping grounds to the many buildings dotting the farm—was meticulously kept. Outside the barn was a large parking lot full of tour buses and empty cars. People smiled and laughed, their arms full of boxes and bags filled with goods.

It had been a few weeks since Taco Tuesday, and Bruce and Rick had been keeping in touch through phone calls. Today, Bruce had decided to bring Rick out to meet his friend Jorge. Rick wasn't entirely sure what they were doing there, and Bruce was keeping quiet with his usual mysterious smile.

Rick jumped out of his car, and Bruce followed more

slowly, his steps shuffling. They were obviously expected because a stocky Hispanic man in his mid-fifties was waiting for them. His dark hair was thinning on top, and he was wearing a short-sleeved, button-down, untucked shirt, long pants, and Birkenstock sandals. He and Bruce shook hands and then pulled in for a half-hug.

"Jorge, this is my grandson, Rick," Bruce said. The two shook hands and exchanged quick pleasantries before Bruce continued. "Jorge is the third generation of a four-generation entrepreneurial family. Before IBC, they owned one business. Now they own four, and they've helped other relatives get started too."

"That's incredible," Rick said with genuine warmth. He knew how hard it was to build a business from the ground up. "Thank you for taking the time to talk to me today."

"Let's see if we can do something special for Rick," Jorge suggested to Bruce. Jorge turned his bright smile and raised eyebrows toward Rick. "Would you like to see behind the scenes of this operation?"

"That would be fantastic!" Rick said.

Jorge led them past the main barn, where visitors were shopping, to a smaller structure beside it. Inside, Jorge's family were packaging and labeling products.

The atmosphere was busy but friendly, with music playing quietly and people laughing and talking in Spanish. A few moms had babies in high chairs or car seats, and there was a feeling of family and community in the air.

Two forklifts anchored the large room, and huge boxes of fruits and nuts from California were stacked in neat rows on the far side of the room. "This is where the real work gets done," Jorge explained. "We unload the fruit there, and at the tables, we sort them into individual bags and packages for sale."

Rick walked along the row of boxes, marveling at the almonds, walnuts, cashews, dried apricots, dates, figs, raisins, and even exotic things like wasabi-covered peas and his favorite, chocolate-covered almonds.

Bruce grabbed a box for Rick. "In case you see anything you want to buy."

Rick nodded. He knew it would be rude to leave empty-handed, but he didn't mind at all. The quality was amazing, and he was happy to support a local business. "How did you start all this?" he asked Jorge.

"Have you heard of Black Wall Street?" When Rick shook his head, Jorge continued. "It was just outside of Tulsa, Oklahoma, in the early 1900s. An African American community with successful doctors, lawyers, and businesses. As a community, they were able to be successful because they figured out the concept of 'buy local.' When people buy within the community, it adds to the overall economy because of higher circulation of dollars." An older woman interrupted Jorge with a string of rapid-fire Spanish that Rick couldn't quite catch. She held up a baby, and Jorge laughed, took the baby in his arms, and kissed it tenderly before answering the woman.

He turned back to Rick, continuing his explanation as Rick browsed. "This community was incredibly profitable at a time when most Black people were living in poverty in the US. They realized that the more times they could get their dollars to cycle through their community, the more their businesses would thrive. So we had the same idea. What if we create a Family Bank, where instead of letting our dollars leak out to credit card companies, banks, student loan companies, you name it, we keep those dollars inside the family and recycle them."

Rick picked up a large bag of pecans and put it in his box. His mom loved to make pecan pie, and he knew she would like the freshness of the product. "So a Family Bank lets you support each other financially."

"Exactly," Jorge said. "First, the older generation

used their pools of capital to pay off the younger generation's debt. Then, the younger generation made the payments they would have been making to the bank on their debt to the older generation. Because it's a Family Bank, the terms of the loans are designed in a way to make it mutually beneficial for all parties. No one is trying to come out on top."

"That's so smart." They had reached the end of the tables, and Rick had grabbed a few more items. A woman came and took the baby from Jorge as he directed Bruce and Rick to the back of the warehouse, taking an ambling pace to match Bruce's slow shuffle.

"Once the family understood how beneficial this could be," Jorge said, "some of them started taking loans from the Family Bank to start their own businesses. The income for the older generation has really increased by becoming 'bankers' for the family, and everyone is doing better."

"IBC has so many different applications," Rick marveled. "You can really use it for any purpose." They arrived at the back of the warehouse, where firewood was stacked almost floor to ceiling.

"As many as you can think of," Bruce said.

"We used it to start another business, selling and installing high-end wood-burning stoves and fireplaces,"

Jorge said. "And see that forklift over there? We bought that by loaning money from our IBC policies to the businesses. Now the businesses make payments to us. Of course, since we control the financing function, we get to decide the terms of the loan."

Bruce nodded. "And because they use IBC policies as their banking system, think about the added windfall that will come in the future through the death benefits."

"That's true, Bruce," Jorge said. "We have tried to start policies insuring as many people as the life insurance company will allow."

"To think a Family Banking system has built so much!" Rick looked around the warehouse and saw how many of Jorge's family were working there. It was truly staggering. "You must be very proud."

Jorge beamed and stuck his thumbs through his belt loops, "You can only imagine."

Rick and his grandfather thanked Jorge for his time and left him to get back to work while they checked out with Rick's purchases. As they walked back to the car, Rick said, "You've taught me so much, but it was great to see it all in action. It really showed just how much you can do."

"I think you're ready," Bruce said as they got into the car.

"Ready for what?"

Bruce handed over a slip of paper. "I learned about IBC from Nash. He's the best in the business. A professional IBC coach. He'll show you the best way to get started."

"Geez. Thanks, Bruce. This is . . ." Rick laughed and slapped the steering wheel. "This is exciting!"

Bruce grinned. "I told you, Rick, I have a gift for picking winners, and I'm banking on you."

A week later, Rick and Meg were sitting at the kitchen table, eating the last of the pecan pie his mother had dropped off the day before. The kids were upstairs doing homework, and the house was peaceful and quiet. The phone rang, and Rick waved Meg back to her seat and got up to answer it.

"Yello?"

"Rick. It's Buddy. I've got . . . some sad news."

"What is it?" Rick sank back into his chair. His heart froze, fearing the worst, knowing without quite knowing what was about to be said.

"It's Dad," Buddy said. "He passed away last night."

"No," Rick said, the word barely a breath. His grandfather was pushing eighty years old, but he was so present, so vibrant. He took up all the space in a room, filling it with warmth. "Oh, Buddy . . ."

Rick jotted down the details of the funeral and passed the phone over to Meg so she could give her condolences too. Then he clasped his hands, bowed his head, and let the tears flow.

Chapter 6

THE MONEY MENTOR

Lesson 6: You Have What it Takes When It Really Matters

The number swam in front of Rick's eyes. Rick's stomach was a clenched fist, his hand trembling. All he could see was grey, the black ink twisting in his sight. He knew the bill would be high, but he had no idea it would be so much.

It had been a month since Bruce passed away. First, there had been the funeral, and then getting his mother sorted out with the funds Bruce had left. Then his son Cooper had broken his wrist playing baseball, and there had been doctor visits and physical therapy. Life had swallowed him up, and now he was staring at a bill that was higher than he expected, and he had no idea how to pay for it.

His beloved Meg said something to him, but he

didn't hear her. She tossed a balled-up cloth napkin at him with a laugh. "Rick! Earth to Rick."

"Dammit! Will you give me some space?" Rick snapped.

"Woah. Where did that come from?" she asked in alarm.

Rick dragged a hand down his face. "I'm sorry. I just . . . Dammit," he said again. He closed the distance between them in a couple long strides, meeting her at the kitchen table, and handed over the bill.

She whistled through her teeth. "That's . . ."

Rick sat down across from her, slumping over the table. "Yeah. It's too much." He dropped his head down on his folded arms, his mind full of numbers. Student loan payments. Credit card debt. Mortgage. Car payments. He already owed $325,000. He was barely managing the minimum payments, making hardly a dent in the principal. And now this bill . . . He had no idea how he was going to pay it.

"I need some air." He stood abruptly and walked out of the kitchen and onto the back deck. He gripped the railing tightly, letting it anchor him, and tilted his face up to the sky. There was a light breeze, and it reminded him of sitting on the patio at La Tropicana with Bruce. As always, thoughts of his grandfather made his chest squeeze tight. They had so little time together. Such a small chance to make the past right, to get to know each other.

"I'm banking on you," he remembered his grandfather saying. That made him think of the card Bruce had given him, the IBC expert who could help him with his finances. He had been too busy to call, but maybe this was exactly the wake-up he needed. Maybe it was time to get serious about IBC.

He walked back inside and kissed Meg on the top of the head. "I'm sorry," he told her again.

She squeezed his hand. "I get it. This is . . . a lot."

"I think I have an answer," he told her. "I need to make a call." He jogged upstairs to the master bedroom and found Nash's contact number on his bedside table. He grabbed the house phone, took a deep breath, and dialed.

"Hello, this is Nash?" a deep voice answered.

"Hi. My name is Rick. I got your number from Bruce before . . . before he passed. I'd like to talk to you about starting an IBC plan," Rick said.

The next afternoon, Rick drove out to Nash's home, which was on a small plot of land just outside of the city center. It had a good view of the farmland beyond and a beautiful screened porch. The IBC expert who

Bruce had introduced to Rick, Nash himself was small in stature, but his silver hair and a strong jaw gave him a very distinguished look. He served Rick lemonade on the porch and chatted about Bruce before they got down to business.

"I helped Bruce set up his IBC banking system. You know he started policies for his boys, and for you when you were born?"

"Yeah, he passed my dad's death benefit on to Shelley, my mom. It's made all the difference. Does that mean I already have a banking system?"

"Well, you have the tools in place. However, having the tool and knowing how to use it are two different things." Rick was reminded of his hammer on the day they worked on Bruce's fence. "When Bruce died, the ownership of the life insurance policies that he set up for you and your children did transfer to you. But you aren't fully aware of the gift Bruce left you. You'll start to understand as you learn how to leverage those policies and begin to make premium deposits into the pool."

"Right. That makes sense." Rick took a sip from his lemonade. The breeze was blowing through the porch screen, and he smiled. "What got you into this whole banking thing?" Rick asked.

"Well, life can throw you some curveballs sometimes.

I was experiencing a few curves in my life and had to make a decision about how I was going to respond. If you can believe it, I was listening to this old recording, "The Strangest Secret." Nash waved a hand through the air to emphasize the words. "It said that you become what you think about, for good or ill. If you believe that you're damaged goods, flawed, forgettable, you become that. If you believe that you're uniquely designed, that you have talents and gifts to share with the world, you become that, too. Well, as I decided to take on those curveballs, this concept of Infinite Banking was laid in my lap and I'm forever grateful."

Nash took a sip from his lemonade, studying Rick over the rim of the glass. "Your grandfather believed that you have a lot to contribute to this world. That there's nobody like you, with your unique talents, gifts, and perspective. He believed you have what it takes . . . and what you have really matters for your family right now."

Rick nodded. The words could have weighed him down, but instead, he found them empowering, uplifting. He did have things to share with the world. He was ready for the challenge ahead. "How do I get started?"

"Well, part of it is spending time around people who truly believe in you. You need your cheerleaders. And you need a purpose."

Rick laughed. "No, I mean, how do I get started in creating my own IBC system?"

"Oh, that," Nash chuckled. "Well, we'll start by having a Dream Conversation with you and Meg. It makes no sense to design an IBC Strategy without knowing what your goals are. So, let's schedule a time to talk. We'll go over the things that make you anxious . . . things you'd like to not have to worry about. We'll talk about the opportunities that get you excited. And then we'll talk about the strengths, talents, and assets that you have access to that you can leverage to accomplish those goals."

"That sounds perfect," Rick said. "Meg loves those types of conversations."

Nash continued, "Ultimately, I want you and Meg to think about and discuss your 'Big Dream.' In other words, when you're both in your 80s and you're looking back over your life together, what is it that you want to have experienced, participated in, or helped create that would make your hearts full of joy? When you know the answer to that, that's your 'Big Dream.' Your banking system may be a key element to making your Big Dream reality."

Rick nodded. He couldn't wait to go home and talk to Meg about his dreams. It had been years since he had let himself think of the future in that way. He knew that he had what it took to make it happen. He didn't have to struggle through life—he could finally create the life he wanted for his family. "I can't wait to start," he said.

That night, after a late family dinner and lots of good conversation, Rick took out the garbage while Meg finished with the dishes. He walked to the curb and chucked the garbage into the can, then tilted his face to the sky. The moon was full and bright overhead, and the trees swayed in a light breeze. Rick felt a peaceful connection to his town, his community, and the people who came before him. Bruce had given him the tools he needed. All he had to do now was pick them up.

Chapter 7

THE FUTURE
UNFOLDING

Lesson 7: Push beyond your
comfort zone.

Sometimes, life feels like long runs of fencing, with
weddings and funerals providing the posts. It certainly
felt like that for Rick when, just a few weeks after
Bruce's death, Buddy's granddaughter announced her
upcoming wedding. Now, six months later, the family
had gathered at Bruce's old farm to celebrate the new
life she was building.

Rick, Meg, and the kids drove down the twisting
road and out to the farmhouse. Rick pointed out a
plane flying overhead, thinking of headwinds and how
his family had finally turned theirs into a tailwind. He
parked the car, and they made their way around the

side of the house to a huge raised deck. Strings of lights stretched from the house to the nearby trees, turning the whole area into a magical grotto. In the distance, Rick could see the fence he had helped Buddy and Bruce fix, still standing proud and strong.

The wedding took place at dusk, and Rick watched the sun setting to the West as the bride and groom exchanged their vows. In sickness and health. For richer for poorer. Rick looked over at Meg with a smile, and she grinned and squeezed his hand. He had a hunch she was thinking of their wedding day, just as he was, and of how far they had come over the last few months. Everything had changed.

After the ceremony, the 150 guests flocked into a huge white barn, which had been decorated for the occasion. Its large double doors had been thrown open to provide a beautiful view of the farm and the rolling hills, and to give easy access to the dance floor set up just inside the doors. Nearby, long buffet tables were loaded with food, and round tables had been placed carefully around the barn for everyone to sit and eat.

Rick and Meg got food and quickly lost their kids to the allure of their cousins and a knot of other children their ages. The adults ate and drank and laughed, catching up with old friends and seeing a lot of new faces. They found Buddy holding court in a corner, proud as a peacock over his family's happiness. Rick congratulated him with a big hug.

"And you've taken over the farm!" Rick said. "Bruce would be so proud of how you've kept it up."

"It's home." Buddy shrugged. "I fit here. What about you? How's the new business going?"

"Really well," Rick said. "I can still remember the day you and Bruce asked me about it, and it sparked something within me. After Nash helped me start up my own IBC system, I had a purpose to work toward. It gave me the courage to get out of my comfort zone. I quit my job the next week!"

"Good for you!" Buddy slapped him on the back.

Distracted by another well-wisher, Buddy stepped away, and Meg left to talk to Buddy's daughter. Rick spotted a group of people at a table in the corner and recognized Mike and Susan from Kevin's wake. Rick had seen them a few times since at IBC community events, and he started to make his way over to them.

He was interrupted in his path by a familiar face: Jonas, a colleague at the university where Rick used to work. Jonas was a tall and lanky adjunct art professor with unruly hair and a boisterous laugh. He and Rick used to bemoan the university's slow pace at implementing new technology when it became available.

"Rick!" Jonas enthusiastically shook Rick's hand. "I haven't seen you in ages!"

"Feels like a lifetime," Rick agreed.

"Did you quit?" Jonas asked.

"I did. Went into business for myself, designing new software for business and some nonprofit use," Rick said. "I especially enjoy working with a foundation that is working toward a cure for diabetes. The work feels very purposeful." The work made Rick feel his dad was watching over him, proud of what he accomplished every day. Rick handed over his card, and Jonas whistled, impressed.

"I've always dreamed of doing something like that," Jonas admitted. "How did you have the courage to start your own business?"

"Well, a lot of it has to do with something called the Infinite Banking Concept," Rick said. "I was just headed over to say hello to some people who use the Infinite Banking Concept, actually. I'd love to introduce you to them."

Remembering his own enthusiasm the first time he made this journey, Rick couldn't help but smile as he led Jonas over to the table. Mike and Susan were there, as well as a few people he hadn't met before. He introduced Jonas to the people he knew, and shared that Mike used IBC to travel the world, while Susan owned mortgages that provided her with passive income.

Mike introduced another couple, friends of Bruce's wife. They had both been teachers in California and deeply in debt. With student loan payments, car payments, and a mountain of credit card debt, they had owed nearly $93,000 on top of their $700,000 mortgage. Bruce convinced them to try IBC, and they were out of debt after only seven years—including that big California mortgage.

"Wow," Jonas said to Rick. "This seems too good to be true. Has it worked for you?"

"You know, I was always taught to follow the conventional path," Rick said. "You know how it is. Get an education, find steady work, invest in your 401(k) retirement plan, pay extra beyond the minimum payment of your credit card debt, save in a 529 plan for your kid's college, have enough for retirement, and don't outlive your money."

"And now?"

"Now, I've used IBC to pursue my dreams. Although it's been only four months, I've completely paid off my consumer debt, and I have a plan to completely pay off my mortgage in four years. Plus, I'm saving for my kids' college tuition in IBC policies that give me guarantees and great flexibility. So yeah, you could say that it's worked for me." He laughed.

Wide-eyed, at a loss for words, Jonas chugged some wine.

Rick grinned. "Do you like tacos?" he asked. "I know this great place in North Lawrence. Their family salsa recipe is amazing."

Later that evening, as the party wound down, Rick took a moment to slip away from the barn. He walked through the fields and out to the fence that he had helped fix not long ago. He ran his fingers over the old wood, thinking about the generations who may stand here, who may perhaps have to fix this very fence again. This farm was a legacy, passing from father to son.

IBC was a legacy, too, one that Bruce had passed down to him, and one that Rick would be able to leave for his children and grandchildren.

A breeze passed overhead, rustling the leaves of the sycamore trees, and Rick smiled. He thought of Bruce and knew his grandfather would be proud. He was part of their legacy now and always would be.

LESSONS LIST

Lesson 1: You are not alone.

Pursuing financial independence can be daunting. However, this isn't a journey that you have to take on your own. Learn from the people around you, those who are on a similar path, and accept help when it's offered. The Infinite Banking Concept creates a financial system for you and future generations. There can be great power in applying the concept with other family members, and don't be afraid to ask a coach for help.

Lesson 2: Life becomes simpler when you control the wind current.

Most Americans are financing their lives on credit cards, bank loans, and other debts, and then paying through the roof on interest rates. Those interest rates feel like a financial headwind that you have to continually fight against. When you control your own pool of money, your own banking system, you can shift that headwind into a tailwind. When you control the pool of money, you can borrow against that pool and control the terms of the loans. You control the "pool rules."

Lesson 3: Get multiple uses of your dollar.

The average person gets only one use from their dollar. They spend it, and they get something for it. When you deposit capital into a whole life insurance policy that's designed to emphasize the cash value, which is the equity, and de-emphasize the death benefit, you gain three uses of your dollars: (1) the death benefit when you pass away, (2) growth that's guaranteed by contract, and (3) loans against your policy to finance anything you want without impacting the growth of the policy.

Lesson 4: Send everything you can to your banking system.

We've all been taught to pay extra on our debt payments. But if you send that extra dollar toward the debt, you're gaining only one use of that money. If you send the minimum payment instead, and put the remaining amount into your IBC system, you'll gain multiple uses of those extra dollars. You can take a loan against the policy and chunk down on the balance of the debt, paying off the same amount, usually sooner, but also strengthening your IBC system.

Lesson 5: Create a Family Bank to recycle money.

A Family Bank lets you support each other. With a Family Bank, all the money to finance expenses, debt, and investments can cycle inside the family system and be reused over and over again. Because it's a Family Bank, the terms of the loans are designed in a way to make it mutually beneficial for all parties. The older generation earns income as bankers, and the younger generation can finance personal needs, as well as new business ventures that will support the next generation too. With a Family Bank, all the money is now cycling inside the system rather than leaking out to other financial institutions, never to be seen again.

Lesson 6: You have what it takes when it really matters.

We all need purpose. Imagine you are nearing the latter years of your life. What is it that you want to have experienced, participated in, or helped create that would fill you with joy and satisfaction? When, after reflection, you know the answer to that question, that's your 'Big Dream.' Your banking system is a key element to making your Big Dream a reality. It may be starting your own business, traveling the world, leaving a legacy for your children—or all three! Once you understand what it is that you're fighting for, you'll be fired up to create the life you want.

Lesson 7: Push beyond your comfort zone.

Taking such a huge step can be intimidating, even scary. When we step outside our comfort zones, there can be fear and stress. However, on the other side of that fear and stress is growth. IBC flies in the face of a lot of conventional financial 'ideas,' but it is worth it. You just need to find the courage to take the first step, learn from those who've done it before you, and make a start. Where you take it from there is limited only by your imagination.

ABOUT THE AUTHOR

Chris Bay inspires financial hope and freedom as an Infinite Banking Concept (IBC) coach at Life Success & Legacy. After serving in the public school system for twenty-two years as a teacher and principal, Bay grew frustrated with his family's  financial circumstances. He and his wife started to ask whether there were tools that could stretch their dollar and make it work harder for them. As a single-income family with an aversion to debt, they found their choices were limited. Then Bay discovered the Infinite Banking Concept.

As Bay began to learn about the Infinite Banking Concept from his IBC coach, Mike Everett, he applied the system to his own life and saw the power and flexibility it provided. Inspired by his love of teaching and his leadership background, Bay knew he wanted to help others understand how to apply the Infinite Banking Concept in their own lives. He became an Authorized Infinite Banking Concept Practitioner with the Nelson Nash Institute and joined Everett as a business partner. As an IBC coach, Bay gains great satisfaction from helping others discover hope and freedom in their financial present, future, and legacy.

Bay lives in Lawrence, Kansas, with his wife, Shawn, their two beautiful and intelligent daughters, Lily and Addie, two cats, three chickens, and one old dog who puts up with the rest.

For many of us, a significant barrier to creating the life we want for ourselves and our families is money. Of course, wisdom tells us financial gain alone is not the answer. With an emphasis on education and developing trusting relationships, our team helps you increase the level of clarity and purpose you have for your life.

We then design a personalized Infinite Banking Concept (IBC) Strategy to support your vision. How do we know this works? Each one of us at Life Success & Legacy was in your shoes at one time learning about the power of IBC. Now, we help others create the life they want.

Visit: https://lifesuccesslegacy.com

FB - facebook.com/lifesuccesslegacy

Twitter - twitter.com/LSL_IBC

Learning Tools:

Contact us - https://lifesuccesslegacy.com/contact-us

Learning Kit - https://lifesuccesslegacy.com/learning-kit

Podcast - https://lifesuccesslegacy.com/podcasts

Order a copy of *Becoming Your Own Banker* by Nelson Nash - https://lifesuccesslegacy.com/store

Order a copy of *The Case for IBC* by Nelson Nash, Carlos Lara, and Robert P. Murphy, PhD - https://life successlegacy.com/store

Register to attend an event - https://lifesuccesslegacy. com/event-registration

Made in the USA
Monee, IL
29 July 2021

74216760R00049